AUGIE
and the MONSTER Thieves

Written by
Gisele Lima

Illustrated by
Jeff West

ISBN: 979-8-9871273-1-5 (Paperback)
ISBN: 979-8-9871273-0-8 (Hardcover)

Written by Gisele Lima
Illustrated by Jeff West
Book design by Misty Black Media LLC
Art Direction by Eric Bross

First printing edition 2023

www.augietheyeti.com

For **Ethan**, who taught me that to find your superpower, you just have to look within.

Special thanks to Eric, Kenneth & Rachel, aka Team Ethan.

Augie the Yeti lived in a world where everyone was different. Big, small, loud, quiet, happy, grumpy. He knew everyone in his neighborhood, and everyone knew him. Augie had

SUPERPOWERS.

Augie was in his room sorting out his collection
of old things. He had worn coins, rusty
spectacles, and old books. There was even an old
pocket watch from his grandfather.

Suddenly, his ears twitched. His super hearing picked up a sound.

"What was that?" Augie wondered.

Was it a cat? No. A squeaky door? No. A badly played guitar? Nope.

He went to his window and focused his super hearing.

"Oh! That's the sound of a girl crying!" Augie concluded.
"Maybe she needs a friend." Augie decided to help.

Augie gathered his things. He packed sunglasses to protect his super eyesight and headphones for his super hearing. He wore a weighted vest that made him feel safe. These gadgets stopped his superpowers from overwhelming him.

After packing extra snacks and a box to store
treasures he might find along the way, Augie
went out into his backyard and through a hole
in the fence.

Augie approached a little girl sitting on her front steps.

"Hello," said the girl.

Augie did not respond right away.

Instead, he looked around. His super-fast brain took everything in. He counted the house's windows. He noticed the colors of the flowers. He smelled the air around him.

1
2
3
4
5
FLOWERS
FIVE
GRASS

"Hello?" said the girl once again.

"Oh, hi!" said Augie. "Sorry. I was distracted by your house. I'm Augie. What's your name?"

"I'm Mila," the girl replied.

"I was in my room when I heard you crying. Are you okay?" Augie asked.

"You heard me from your room? How? You must have super hearing!" said Mila.

"Actually, I do," Augie told her. "I'm Autistic. I have powerful senses. What made you sad?"

"I lost my grandma's necklace, and I can't find it anywhere," Mila said tearfully.

Augie understood. He imagined losing his grandfather's pocket watch and knew how upset he would feel. "Don't worry, Mila. I'll help you look for your necklace. Where did you see it last?"

"I think it was on the kitchen table," replied Mila.

A loud lawnmower started up somewhere. Augie winced.
Varoom!
He was glad he had his headphones on.
He flapped his hands and wrinkled his nose to help him concentrate over the loud noise and the strong smell of cut grass.

"If you think you lost it in the house, why are you out here?" asked Augie.

"You're going to think I'm silly, but I think **monsters** took it!" Mila whispered. "I hear weird noises late at night coming from there!" She pointed to her backyard.

Augie could see that the path led into the woods.

"Monsters, huh?" Augie took a deep breath and felt his vest hold him tight. The vest reminded him that he was safe and made him feel calm. "Let's go check in the woods!" he suggested.

"My parents say I'm not allowed to go into the forest," said Mila in a wobbly voice.

"Well, nobody told me I'm not allowed to go there," Augie replied. "I'm going to help you."

Augie walked toward the trees and entered the forest.

The lawnmower had stopped, which meant that Augie could remove his headphones and use his super senses to focus on the many sounds and smells around him.

He could definitely smell something. Was it an animal? Was it a monster?

Augie scanned the ground, looking for patterns and clues.

Hmm. I see footprints, but they don't look like monster prints, he thought.

As Augie came out of the forest, something hit him.

He used his super speed to race out of the forest
and back into Mila's yard.

"What was that?" asked Mila, holding a trashcan lid as a shield.

"I think I know what it is!" replied Augie. "The tracks, the smell, the bits of trash. It's not a monster. It's just . . ."

"Do you think they took my necklace?" asked Mila.

"There's only one way to find out," said Augie. "Let's make a plan! What do we know about raccoons?"
"They make a mess of trash and look like bandits. They can be sneaky, smelly, and a little bit scary. And they have sharp teeth!" said Mila.
"BINGO!" shouted Augie.
"Sharp teeth?" Mila shivered.
Augie nodded. "They love food. They won't be able to resist the smell of my cheesy snacks!"

Augie and Mila ventured into the woods. Mila held her shield, and Augie had his bag of cheesy crackers. They climbed over logs and ducked under branches. All they had to do was find the raccoon's den.

Augie's super hearing picked up a
faint crunching noise.

Mila had stepped on a candy wrapper.

"Look!" Augie pointed to a trail of
trash leading to . . .

Augie poured cheesy crackers on the ground not far from the den. He and Mila hid behind a tree, waiting to see if the bait would work.

Soon, they heard a rustling sound. Raccoons raced out of the den! Augie and Mila hurried to inspect it.

Augie reached
into the den.

He pulled something out. **"MY NECKLACE!"** shouted Mila.

"Thank you, Augie! Without your help and superpowers, I would never have found it!"

Augie **SMILED.**

"Today, I've battled monsters . . .

found treasure . . .

. . . and made a **new friend."**

GISELE LIMA is a proud mom to her son Ethan, who inspires her to tell stories that raise awareness and help empower those on the Autism Spectrum. Originally from Brazil, she now resides in Los Angeles, California, with her son, their guinea pigs Mario & Luigi, and their hamster Brenda.

www.ingramcontent.com/pod-product-compliance
Lightning Source LLC
Chambersburg PA
CBHW040224110726
48007CB00009B/170